The Deep Things of God

Jeff Kliewer

Grammatical editing by Janet Bishop

Theological editing by Paulo Freire

Cover Art by Berend de Kort, Tilburg, Netherelands, Pexels.com

ISBN: B08W7DMTCB

DEDICATION

To Cornerstone Church. It was your call to the pastorate that brought me before the Evangelical Free Church council in defense of my theology. It was that occasion that forced me to write this content. And had you not desired to participate further, were you always content to swim only in shallow waters, I would have found no occasion to turn that content into a book. You hold here in your hands a product of your desire to know Him more.

CONTENTS

ACKNOWLEDGEMENTS

I am very grateful for The Evangelical Free Church of America. They have provided the Church at large with one of the best Statements of Faith ever written. While visiting a non-EFCA church in Florida, I glanced at their Statement of Faith and immediately recognized it as our own. With permission, they had adopted the EFCA Statement, and I think they were wise to do so. It would be very hard to improve upon. I especially want to express my thanks to Paulo Freire, Pastor of Hope EFC in New Jersey and a member of the Board of Ministerial Standing with the EFCA. He invested many hours in making my ordination paper better. The Deep Things of God is that paper turned into a book.

INTRODUCTION

A grown man won't be satisfied with a bowl of milk. A second-amendment guy won't be satisfied with an air-soft gun. A deep-sea diver won't be satisfied with a swimming pool. And a mature Christian won't be satisfied with the milk-bottle, play-pistol, shallow-water theology of today's Evangellyfish[1] religion.

The Bible's theology is "strong meat" (Hebrews 5:12 KJV), a "two-edged sword" (Hebrews 4:12), and "deep waters" (Proverbs 18:4). Why be content with only that which is fit for a child? We all begin as babies in Christ, so there is no shame in starting there. But having no desire to grow up would be a problem.

When Paul "decided to know nothing among you except Jesus Christ and Him crucified" (1 Corinthians 2:2), he spoke of the

---

[1] Doug Wilson coined the term in his 2012 book "Evangellyfish" https://canonpress.com/products/evangellyfish-hbk/

starting point of faith. He was determined to leave everything superfluous, even theological precepts, off to the side until the main thing could first be established. Unnecessary baggage might prevent unbelievers from hearing the essential things that are able to make a person wise unto salvation (2 Timothy 3:15).

But Paul didn't intend to leave everything except the gospel off to the side forever. He went on to say that "among the mature we do impart wisdom" (1 Corinthians 2:6). These things—wisdom for the mature—are what Paul then describes as "the deep things of God" (1 Corinthians 2:10 KJV). Hence, the title of this book. As a "scribe" entrusted with God's Word, like a homeowner displaying treasures new and old that we keep inside our house (Matthew 13:52), I wrote this book that we might know Him (Philippians 3:10), and knowing Him we might press on to know Him more (Philippians 3:12-14). "Let those of us who are mature think this way" (Philippians 3:15a).

We who are mature think about the deep things of God, and that in no way involves outgrowing the gospel. If to evangelize we must set aside the deep things of God, the reverse is not also true. To wade into the deep things of God we do not set aside the gospel. The gospel is more like the waters of an ocean. As soon as you set your foot into the surf of the beach, you are touching gospel water, and however deeply you swim in the depths of that ocean, it's all the same water. "Christ and Him crucified" (1 Co. 2:2) is always and everywhere the living water in which we swim.

The gospel has five points that must be accepted if anyone is to be in the ocean of God's saving grace. First, there is the person of Christ. Jesus is the Messiah, the Son of God, Almighty God, and truly human (Matthew 16:15-16). Second, there is the work of Christ. Jesus died on the cross to satisfy God's wrath against sinners and He rose from the dead on the third day (Acts 2:23-24). Third, there is the Scripture. The ground upon which sinners are held responsible to believe the gospel is the Bible—that is: the good news is "according to the scriptures" (1 Corinthians 15:3-4). Fourth, there is forgiveness of sin and eternal life. The good promise is that all sins will be forgiven and everlasting life will be imparted (Luke 24:47). Fifth, there is repentance and faith. The ones receiving what was promised are those who turn away from sin in turning to Christ, trusting Him and Him alone to save from the just deserts of sin (Mark 1:15). These 5 things are the gospel.

The gospel is never to be filed away in the been-there, done-that category of our thinking. It is ever to be on our minds and on our lips. As we dive now into the deep things of God, consider yourself swimming in the gospel, immersed in an ocean called grace.

CHAPTER 1

GOD

We believe in one God, Creator of all things, holy, infinitely perfect, and eternally existing in a loving unity of three equally divine Persons: the Father, the Son and the Holy Spirit. Having limitless knowledge and sovereign power, God has graciously purposed from eternity to redeem a people for Himself and to make all things new for His own glory.

—EFCA Statement of Faith

That God is Creator is definitional to His being (Gen. 1:1, John 1:1, Rev. 22:13). Unlike everything other than Him (Is. 43:10-11), He has no beginning, but simply is who He is. He depends on nothing or no one to have existence (Ex. 3:14). Therefore He is rightfully the One to whom all glory is always due, since He alone is from everlasting to everlasting (Psalm 90:2).

God alone is able to speak things into existence *ex nihilo*, which He did, according to what seems to be the plainest reading of Genesis 1 and Exodus 20:11, in six literal days. God rested on the seventh day (Genesis 2:2), not because He had grown tired (1 Kings 18:27), but because He was setting a pattern of six-day work and one-day rest for people to follow (Genesis 2:3, Exodus 20:8-11). The Sabbath is also a picture of the rest believers find in Christ (Heb. 4:9).

Regard for the Scripture as the fully inspired Word of God and the corollary doctrine of inerrancy commends this view of a literal six-day creation. While it may not be of utmost importance to hold to a young-earth view of creation, it matters entirely whether or not one believes the text, interpretational issues notwithstanding. The flow of the text reads most naturally as a literal six days, so this view is to be commended.

God has essential attributes. These are what would still be true of God in any imaginable world. For example, His wrath is not an essential attribute, since a world in which sin never existed would not include anything against which God would carry wrath. We speak of essential attributes for the purpose of knowing God as He revealed the Essence of Himself to be (Romans 1:21, Psalm 19). God is uncreated (John 1:1), omnipotent (Daniel 4:35), omnipresent (Psalm 139:7-12), omniscient (John 1:48), eternal (Psalm 90:2) spirit (John 4:24).

Regarding His moral attributes, God is love (1 John 4:8); He is kind, merciful, gracious, slow to anger, and faithful (Exodus 34:6), but also wrathful toward sin (Revelation 6:17). It is necessary and important to understand the eternal nature and divine power of God (Romans 1:21) because such an understanding properly upholds God as the true center of all things. A God-centered worldview honors Him as Lord of all (1 Peter 3:15). Man-centered worldviews are woefully insufficient because they attempt to rob God of His glory (Is. 48:1-11).

The holiness of God is the sum of His attributes (Isaiah 6:3, Revelation 4:8). To be "holy" means to be "set apart". God is set apart from all created things because He exists in the uniqueness of His incommunicable attributes and in the perfection of His morality. God's holiness is the fixed point in the universe that gives meaning to the very concept of morality and goodness. His holiness is the reason that everything sinful stands condemned (John 3:18).

That God is One, according to "the Shema" of Israel, stated in Deuteronomy 6:4 and affirmed by Jesus in Mark 12:29, refers to the very essence, the being, of God. Yet, within this monotheism, God is not unitarian. There are, in fact, three divine Persons that are rightfully called God (Matthew 28:19, 1 Corinthians 12:4-6). Each member of this three-in-one being possesses all the attributes of deity. None are creations in any way. Each member is eternal, all-powerful, and rightfully called "God" (1 Corinthians 8:6, John 8:58, Acts 5:3-4). The Father is not the Son or Spirit, etc. Yet each member of the Trinity is properly God.

As three equally divine persons, God exists in a loving unity. Because there is a distinction between the Persons, there is always an Object of love; each Person eternally exists and eternally loves the other two persons. That is how it can be said that "God is love" (1 John 4:8). But the eternal unity between the persons goes beyond relational dynamics to the very ontology of God. He is not three gods; He is one being, one essence.

A contemporary denial of the Trinity is Oneness Pentecostalism and particularly the brand espoused by Philadelphia's Gino Jennings, with whom I have contended in recent years. Jennings' view is Socinian/Modalistic. It is heretical because it denies distinction between the Persons of the Trinity. These distinctions are Scriptural (John 1:1, John 17:5, Revelation 1:1, Revelation 22:16, Hebrews 1:2). To deny them is to attack the attributes of God. That is why teachings like these must be condemned (2 Corinthians 11:3-4, Romans 16:17, Titus 1:9).

God has limitless knowledge, and there is never a need for God to learn anything. He does not even discover things as they unfold in history, but knows the ends from the beginning because He ordains them and stands beyond time (Psalm 139:2, Ephesians 1:11). God is sovereignly powerful as King and has the ability to bring to pass whatsoever He desires to do, which is, in fact, what comes to pass (Acts 4:27-28, Is. 10, Gen. 50:20). Since limitless knowledge and sovereign power are definitional to God's essence, to know Him as Lord and Savior includes this affirmation of His eternal power and divine nature (Rom. 1:20), even if we can only understand such infinity like one who looks at it through a dark glass (1 Co. 13:12).

That God graciously purposes from eternity to redeem a people for Himself is merely the application of this doctrine of God having a decree (Ephesians 1:11) in the area of soteriology (Ephesians 1:5). The doctrine of election is significant because it teaches us that God saves sinners without help and is purifying this chosen people to be zealous for good works (Titus 2:14). God's plan of salvation is grace plus nothing.

God's intent is to redeem a *people*. This present earth, by contrast, is stored up for fire (2 Peter 3:7). Therefore Christians ought not be overly consumed with environmentalism, although we ought to be good stewards of creation (Genesis 1:28). The creation groans until the day comes for it to be set free (Romans 8:20-21).

CHAPTER 2

THE BIBLE

We believe that God has spoken in the Scriptures, both Old and New Testaments, through the words of human authors. As the verbally inspired Word of God, the Bible is without error in the original writings, the complete revelation of His will for salvation, and the ultimate authority by which every realm of human knowledge and endeavor should be judged. Therefore, it is to be believed in all that it teaches, obeyed in all that it requires, and trusted in all that it promises.

–EFCA Statement of Faith

The canon of Scripture is not the gift of the Church to her people but the gift of God to the Church (2 Timothy 3:16). Although refutation of gnostic and other counterfeits (2 Corinthians 10:4-5) required synods in 393 and 397 to affirm what the Church had always known to be apostolic (Acts 1:25), consistent with other

Old and New Testament doctrine (Deuteronomy 13:1-3), and universally recognized by the churches (1 Corinthians 15:5-11), those synods did not create the canon. Athanasius listed the 27 books of the New Testament earlier that century. Origen preceded him. Clement in 97 AD referenced 13 NT books in his letter to the Corinthians. Even Peter in a New Testament book acknowledged Paul's epistles as Scripture equal to the Old Testament (2 Peter 3:16). It was God who created the canon of 66 books.

There are variants in the textual tradition. For example, Mark 16:9-20 and John 7:53-8:11 are probably late introductions. Since we cannot be certain that these passages, or the Comma Johanneum (1 John 5:7), are inspired, we should not establish doctrine upon them or use them polemically in our apologetic battles. However, we cannot be certain that they were not inspired, so they ought to be included in translations and footnoted as questionable. But like a thousand piece jigsaw puzzle with one thousand and ten pieces in the box, we have the original pieces, even if we have ten other pieces that have worked their way into the textual tradition. Scholars who specialize in textual criticism are able to reproduce the original Hebrew, Greek and Aramaic texts with a very high level of certainty at any particular point. And, where there are points of disagreement, no major doctrine hangs in the balance since the theology of the Bible is determined by the whole of Scripture (Romans 3:28, James 2:24).

There are many false teachers who include books like Jasher in the canon. I respond to them by pointing out that what they call Jasher was written only 500 years ago by an anti-Trinitarian polemicist. By appealing to this pseudo-Jasher, anti-Trinitarians hope to show that the "us" of Genesis 1:26 and 11:3 refers to God and angels, and is therefore not a Trinitarian reference. It is therefore important to demonstrate that such forgeries are not the original Jasher referred to in Scripture (Joshua 10:13).

Like the Son of God, who is fully human and fully divine, all Scripture is at the same time the human product of human minds (Luke 1:1-4) and the divine product of God's omniscient mind (Psalm 119, 2 Timothy 3:16). Because the Scripture was given in human language, we have the ability to adequately understand the meaning of the Scriptures. Our path to understanding is simply that of a careful reader. Our job is to "think the author's thoughts after him" by accepting the plain meaning of words within their historical and grammatical context.

Because God spoke through the human authors (the Scriptures are the very breath of God, 2 Timothy 3:16), we have grounds for accepting the inerrancy of the Scriptures. Since the author's writings were carried along by the Holy Spirit (2 Peter 1:21), they are not *merely* a human product, but are, in fact, the very words of God. God's verbal inspiration allows for God's very words, not just inspired ideas, to be *revealed* to us in Scripture through miracles, prophetic utterances, historical narrative, and poetry in the Old Testament and supremely through Jesus Christ in the New Testament (Hebrews 1:1). The Holy Spirit *illuminates* our understanding, person by person, to see what is already there in the text (1 Corinthians 2:10-16), but the revelation itself remains steadfast as the minds of individuals are illumined to it. We can understand the Scriptures by a historical grammatical hermeneutic. Because of the Scriptures' divine origin, we can trust them in everything they teach.

The Old Testament is to be regarded as inspired by God in the same way as we regard the New Testament—plenary verbal inspiration (Romans 3:2). The Old Testament reveals the same God and the same plan of salvation by grace as is revealed in the New Testament. However, like a dimly lit room that is full of furniture, the Old Testament is shadowy about some things that are obvious in the New Testament. The Tri-unity of God, for example, is revealed somewhat in the Old Testament, but it shines forth in radiant light in the New Testament. In that sense, revelation is progressive (Ephesians 3:6).

The plenary verbal inspiration of the Scriptures extends only as far as the autographs of each of the 66 books of the Bible. As would be expected after the passing of thousands of years, we do not have any of the originals. Nevertheless, we see it clearly demonstrated in the textual records that God has preserved His Word throughout the ages (Matthew 5:18, Matthew 24:35).

The New Testament has more ancient attestation than any other work from antiquity. All the books of the OT canon were always regarded by Israel to be Scripture (Romans 3:2). When the Apostles oversaw the writing of the New Testament, all of these 27 books were regarded by the Church to be Scripture. Peter even affirms Paul's letters as being Scripture when he wrote his own epistle (2 Peter 3:16).

Given the reliability of the modern English translations that we have, such as the ESV, the NASB, the NKJV, based as they are upon the most reliable manuscripts, and given that the autographs were fully inspired by God, it should go without saying that we can trust what God has preserved for us. Thus, the Scriptures continue to have *ultimate authority* over our lives, which means that everything the Bible affirms is completely true and binding (Isaiah 40:8).

Practically, the inerrancy of Scripture means that the Bible has no contradictions, mistakes, or internal inconsistencies in the original manuscripts. The infallibility of Scripture notes that the Bible always proves trustworthy to those who stand upon it (Isaiah 55:10-11). The authority of Scripture teaches that the Bible has full rights over us, and never the other way around (John 10:35). These doctrines affect all areas of ministry. In his study, the pastor must exegete the Scriptures (Psalm 119:97), drawing out the author's intended meaning, being careful not to import meaning that was not already in the text. Coming out of the study and into the pulpit, the preacher must exposit what the text says, not preach his own opinion (1 Timothy 4:7). The teacher must equip students to likewise exegete the Scriptures (2 Timothy 2:2). The counselor must find the passages of Scriptures that address every area of human neediness, rather than running off to secular psychology and medicine. The one who trains leaders must equip others to wield the sword of Scripture rather than the tools of men (Hebrews 4:12). If we have the very Word of God, then His Word must form the basis of all our ministry (Acts 20:27).

We live in a day when even some professing evangelicals who claim to agree with the doctrine of inerrancy are expressing doubts about inerrancy. Nevertheless, it remains, and always shall remain, that the Scriptures are inerrant (John 10:35, 1 Peter 1:24-25, Isaiah 40:8).

By general revelation God reveals Himself to all people, even without the Bible, through nature, logic, and the senses. General revelation provides enough awareness of God to condemn (Romans 1:20-21) but not enough to save (Romans 3:9-20). Special revelation is that which is revealed in Scripture (Deuteronomy 29:29). It reveals the way to be saved (Acts 16:31) and everything we need to know for life and godliness (2 Peter 1:3).

In a postmodern culture where frontal attacks against a person's faith are discouraged, because personal beliefs are considered to always be valid for the person, it is often the perspicuity of Scripture that comes under attack. Scripture is derided by asserting that any number of interpretations of a passage are equally valid. But interpretations divested from the Author's intent are a twisting (2 Peter 3:16) of Scripture, often to tickle ears (2 Timothy 4:3), not valid interpretation, because the Scriptures are not only true but clear (1 Samuel 15:14).

Because of the sufficiency of Scripture the Word is able to stand alone without help from any other authority to do such things as reveal God, open the way of salvation, direct the Church, and provide a rule of faith. We ought not look for new prophecies to compete with Scripture, because the canon is already sufficient and complete. Likewise, aberrant religious movements, such as Roman Catholicism, set up other seats of authority, making them equal to Scripture. But in truth, Scripture is sufficient, over and against whatever man sets up. However, believing in Sola Scriptura does not imply that learning from other books or people is out of bounds. Scripture is "the ultimate authority by which every realm of human knowledge and endeavor should be judged". In other words, Scripture—not human reasoning or any other thing—is the epistemological foundation of the Christian.

The Word of God is to be believed in all that the authors intended to teach. For example, when Scripture mentions a "sunset", the author does not intend to say that the sun literally went down vis-a-vi the earth, but only that there was a sunset, as used idiomatically. The Scripture is to be obeyed, without qualification, in all it commands, according to the New Covenant under which we live, and the general equity and moral guidance we receive from the Old. Scripture is to be trusted in all that it affirms because the Scriptures are the very words of God (2 Peter 1:20). The implication for my life and ministry is that I am solemnly charged to preach the Word of God in season and out of season (2 Timothy 4:2) and to never turn to the right or left of it (Proverbs 4:27).

CHAPTER 3

THE HUMAN CONDITION

We believe that God created Adam and Eve in His image, but they sinned when tempted by Satan. In union with Adam, human beings are sinners by nature and by choice, alienated from God, and under His wrath. Only through God's saving work in Jesus Christ can we be rescued, reconciled, and renewed.
*   –EFCA Statement of Faith*

Adam and Eve were created in the "Imago Dei", meaning that humanity bears a likeness to God in our intellect, will, emotions, authority, and ability to relate to God (Genesis 1:26-27). We are not ontologically the same being as God, nor could we ever be like Him in that regard (Isaiah 43:10-11), because the uncreated Creator is utterly unique (Psalm 90:2). But He created us with attributes that bear resemblance to His communicable attributes in ways that lesser beasts of the earth do not bear resemblance. Our minds are able to process complex thoughts. We are able to make significant and real moral choices (Isaiah 10:7). Our emotions are wide ranging and capable of the highest heights and lowest depths (Job 3:11). Most importantly, we are able to relate to God, receiving words from Him and offering Him our prayers (Ephesians 6:18), even as God Himself has capacity to communicate one member of the Trinity to another. We are able to glorify Him through His saving work in Christ Jesus, and we are able to enjoy Him forever (Psalm 16:11). The implication of this doctrine is that all people, regardless of religion, behavior, age, self-awareness, or any other thing, have intrinsic value and ought to be treated accordingly. This is the basis of natural rights.

Satan is that angel whom God created to worship Him but who fell in rebellion (Isaiah 14:12-15, Ezekiel 28:11-19). He tempted Adam and Eve in the Garden of Eden (Genesis 3), and he tempts people today (1 Peter 5:8-9). He is working to overtake God and rule the world (1 Corinthians 4:4), but his effort will fail (Revelation 20:10).

At the fall of humanity (Genesis 3), Adam fell into sin and all of humanity fell into sin with him (Romans 5:12-14). Adam was our federal head. From that moment on, Adam's last name could well have been "Sinner", and all people inherit from him the guilt of that title. Jesus Christ is the exception to this rule, abnormally born by conception through the Holy Spirit (Luke 1:35). In contrast to Jesus' sinless perfection, we are totally depraved (Romans 3), even dead in sin (Ephesians 2:1). Whereas we may not do the most wicked things imaginable, even our best deeds are tinged with sin (Isaiah 64:6). Apart from Christ, we are helplessly lost in our total depravity. Sin is lawlessness (1 John 3:4). Sin is rebellion against God (Isaiah 1:2).

It is not the case that we can blame Adam for giving us a sin nature. Rather, if any of us were in his position, we would have likewise eventually fallen. We are sinners by nature (Romans 3:23). Moreoever, in our actual lives, the same sad reality plays out, person by person. Every individual rejects the right and chooses the wrong (Isaiah 7:16).

Because of sin, man is alienated from God. Relationship with God is broken. Being estranged, there is need for reconciliation, which is what our Mediator Jesus Christ is able to provide (2 Corinthians 5:18). We stand in need of grace, hopeless unless God elects us to be saved, because the natural man does not even desire God (Romans 8:7).

Thus, the wrath of God is His intense burning anger against sin, and not only against sin, but also against the sinners (Psalm 5:5, 11:5) who perpetrate such an affront to His holiness (Isaiah 6:3-5). It is not only the Father, but also the Son (Revelation 6:17) and, by implication, the Spirit, who have wrath toward sin and sinners.

The human condition is desperate. Each of us needs *rescue*, meaning that there is no resource inside of ourselves to save us. We are rescued from the wrath of God by the crushing of the Son (Isaiah 53:10). We need *salvation* from without. Every human needs *reconciliation*, meaning that we are born enemies of God, a stench to His nostrils on account of our putrid sinfulness; we are broken in relationship to Him. We are reconciled to God by the shedding of Jesus' blood (2 Corinthians 5:18, 1 Peter 3:18). Each of us needs *renewal*, meaning that the life we had in the flesh was really death (Ephesians 2:1). Although our bodies work, each one is returning to the dust from whence we came. We need new life because we are totally depraved. Thanks be to God through Jesus Christ our Lord, we have rescue, reconciliation, and renewal! It can never be overstated that only Jesus Christ can meet these needs of ours.

CHAPTER 4

JESUS CHRIST

We believe that Jesus Christ is God incarnate, fully God and fully man, one Person in two natures. Jesus—Israel's promised Messiah—was conceived through the Holy Spirit and born of the virgin Mary. He lived a sinless life, was crucified under Pontius Pilate, arose bodily from the dead, ascended into heaven and sits at the right hand of God the Father as our High Priest and Advocate.

—EFCA Statement of Faith

The eternally existent Son became flesh at his incarnation. He was already the Son before creation (Hebrews 1:2), but He took on flesh (John 1:14). The name Jesus was given to Him on the eighth day after his birth (Luke 2:21). It was necessary that the Son of God become a man to save men (Hebrews 2:16) because only then could He bridge the gap between God and men. He had to die as a man in order to function as our representative and substitute (2 Corinthians 5:21).

Jesus Christ is one person of the Trinity. The one person Jesus Christ is infinitely greater than anything in creation. There is nothing in creation that adequately compares to Him. Unlike any other person that we as creatures may encounter, Jesus the Creator actually has two natures that coexist in a Hypostatic Union. When the Son took on human flesh, He added a human nature to His personhood, which from all eternity had only a divine nature. Nothing of the divine nature was lost in the transaction. Nor were the two natures mixed together, like a tablet dissolving in liquid. Rather, through this Hypostatic Union, the full extent of both natures now and eternally exist together in the one person. This does not affect God's immutability because He has not changed His divine nature by adding flesh.

The incarnation did not empty Jesus of any of His divine attributes. Nevertheless, as Philippians 2:7 reveals, it was inexpressibly humble for the second member of the Trinity to take on human attributes. It is important to note that the Son actively *considered* and decided not to grasp after the benefits of equality with the Father. The activity of considering can only be done by a person who already exists. This person laid aside the comforts of heaven and the worship of angels to suffer things that humans do, like cold, painful relationships, injuries, hunger (Luke 4:2) and death (Matthew 27). The miracles that Jesus was able to perform while in the flesh were empowered by the Holy Spirit, but just as much so, they were prerogatives of Jesus, something He was able to do, since He has never ceased being God (Philippians 2:7, Hebrews 1:8).

That it would be the second member of the Trinity who would take on human flesh was partially revealed in the Old Testament (Genesis 1:26, Psalm 2, Psalm 110), but that an anointed one (Messiah) would come from Abraham's seed to bless Israel, and indeed the whole world (Genesis 12:1-3), was a robust promise. A full-orbed expectation of Messiah's coming developed from all 39 books of the Old Testament. Jesus fulfills every promise, either having already done so in His first appearing or being sure to do so in His second coming. It is important to see Jesus as Israel's promised Messiah because it allows all of the Scripture to inform our understanding of who Jesus is, and it retains continuity between New and Old Testaments.

It was essential that Messiah be incarnate deity, virgin born and sinless. That Israel's promised Messiah be more than just a man whom God raises up to save humanity, but even the very God Himself clothed as He was in human flesh, adding to His divinity a human nature, is essential to His plan of salvation. Because Jesus Christ is fully God, God bears the suffering owed to sinners and through propitiation satisfies His own anger by meeting His own demands for justice. As fully human, the substitute who bears the penalty owed to humanity is truly able to represent us and stand in our stead (Romans 5:17).

The virgin birth was essential because the seed of the woman (Genesis 3:15), from which Jesus came, provided full humanity for Him, yet being through the unique means of conception by the Holy Spirit, Adam's sin was not imputed to this holy offspring (Romans 5:12, Luke 1:35). That Jesus be sinless when He lay down His life was essential because only a perfect substitute can take away the iniquity of sinners (2 Corinthians 5:21). Otherwise, He would have had to die for His own sin (Romans 6:23). Praise

God for coming in the flesh, being born without a sin nature, and living a sinless life in order to be righteous and impute that righteousness (2 Corinthians 5:21) to us through His dying and rising! Although Jesus was already righteous before incarnation, His Law-keeping, all His active obedience, as a human, not just His passive obedience in willingly laying down His life (John 10:18), is part of the righteousness that He was then able to impute to us through His dying and rising.

It was not possible for Jesus to have sinned (Hebrews 6:18). The difference between physical ability and moral ability explains why this is the case. Jesus was physically able to do whatever a temptation proposed for Him to do. But because He is God and His nature is purer than the brightness of the purest light (John 1:4, Revelation 21:23), there was nothing in His nature to desire evil and everything in His nature to desire good. It is not possible for a person whose essential attributes are the definition of goodness to do evil.

Jesus died for the sins of the elect (John 10:11), not for His own sins, which were none (1 Peter 2:22). He died in our place (1 Peter 3:18, Isaiah 53:10, 2 Corinthians 5:21).

37

Another important event as it pertains to the Hypostatic Union of two natures in the one person of Jesus Christ was the resurrection, by which we are justified (Romans 4:25, see page 44). Christ's resurrection body was the same real physical body that Joseph and Nicodemus laid in the tomb (John 19:38). Jesus did not merely rise spiritually. He never ceased to exist, for it is impossible for the Creator/Sustainer to cease to exist (Colossians 1:15-20). The body that rose was the flesh that was buried, but it was also changed, made imperishable, capable of things that natural bodies are not able to do (1 Corinthians 15:42-49).

After forty days of making appearances to His disciples, Jesus was taken up into heaven, a cloud hiding His body from their sight (Acts 1:9). In heaven, Jesus sat down at the right hand of the Father (Hebrews 10:12). This sitting is a picture of Jesus' authoritative rule (Psalm 110, the most quoted passage in the New Testament). It also pictures Jesus in communication (in perfect agreement) with the Father, where He is able to plead for His children as their High Priest (Hebrews 7:25) and Advocate (Psalm 110:4, 1 John 2:1). The basis of His intercession for us is His finished work on the cross, where atonement was made. Tetelestai (John 19:30).

Jesus' High Priesthood and advocacy for me is the basis for my life and ministry (1 John 2:1), for I have no standing before the Father without it. The blood of Jesus not only forensically justified me at the moment of my justification (Romans 3:24), but going forward, His blood continues to cleanse my conscience from acts that lead to death (Hebrews 9:14). Ministers are able to stand and speak for God (1 Peter 4:11), not because we are worthy of such a thing, but because we have a High Priest and Advocate with the Father.

CHAPTER 5

THE WORK OF CHRIST

We believe that Jesus Christ, as our representative and substitute, shed His blood on the cross as the perfect, all-sufficient sacrifice for our sins. His atoning death and victorious resurrection constitute the only ground for salvation.
—EFCA Statement of Faith

The gospel is all about the person and work of Jesus Christ (Revelation 1:1). Only Jesus in His full humanity and full deity can bridge the gap to bring us to God (1 Peter 3:18). The only way for Him to have brought us to God was through His atoning work and resurrection (1 Corinthians 15:3-4) because, in our union with Christ (Ephesians 1:3-14), He dies our death and His life becomes life to us (Colossians 3:4).

As representing a new humanity—a people for God's own possession (Titus 2:14)—Jesus perfectly obeys the will of the Father, not only as one obedient Son, but as the one Son who acts on behalf of His people, this new humanity. As our substitute (2 Corinthians 5:21), He took the believers' place when He died on the cross. It is a death penalty owed to us (Genesis 2:17), yet in a great exchange, He is the one punished in our stead. The Good Shepherd laid down His life for His sheep—the elect of God (John 10:11, 2 Timothy 1:9).

The blood of Jesus needed to be shed because life is in the blood and God has given it upon the altar to make atonement for sins (Leviticus 17:11, 1 John 2:2, Hebrews 9:22). The cross on which Jesus died was the place of the sacrifice that God had ordained for our sin debt to be paid. Therefore, the message of Christ's dying is called "the word of the cross" (1 Corinthians 1:18). It is essential to hold that the cross is central to salvation because without the cross we have no life in us (John 6:53). The accomplishment of redemption was by sheer grace (Eph. 1:6).

Christ's sacrificial death is perfect because it leaves nothing for which we have to atone. He pays our sin debt in full (John

19:30). The cross is therefore all-sufficient. It completely meets our need for redemption (2 Peter 1:3). The value of Jesus' death is infinite (1 Peter 1:19), having more than enough value than what was necessary to atone for every sin ever committed, and atoning for the sins of everyone for whom it was intended (John 6:39, John 10:28, John 17:9). He provided for His elect precisely what we needed (Ephesians 1:3).

Those who have a wider hope of salvation beyond Christ and His work entertain a vain notion. The horror of sin was so severe it required payment in the blood of the Son (Leviticus 17:11, Hebrews 9:23). If there were another way, then surely God would not have been pleased to crush His own Son (Matthew 26:39, Isaiah 53:10).

Through the atonement, the reparation for a wrong or injury required by the one offended is fully made. God required an atoning sacrifice to reconcile us to Himself (Exodus 30:10). As our penal substitute, Jesus' death expiates our sin. Thus He removes our guilt and our debt (Psalm 103:12). His death propitiates the wrath of God (1 John 2:2), so that the Father's wrath is turned away from us entirely and absorbed by Jesus Christ. The wrath is spent. The Father accepts Jesus' death as being satisfactory (Isaiah 53:10-11, 1 Peter 3:18). The divine demands of justice are likewise satisfied (Romans 3:26).

Redemption is the purchasing back of sinners like us from slavery to sin (Ruth 4:1-10, Hosea 3:2). The price having been paid, we are then reconciled to God. There no longer remains any animosity from God toward us. Grace has met our need. There shall never be condemnation (Romans 8:1). We are forever regarded as friends (John 15:15).

There are three significant imputations in the Bible. Adam's sin was imputed to all his descendants (Romans 5:12-14). On the cross, the sin of the elect was imputed to Christ (Deuteronomy 21:23, Galatians 3:13). Through faith, Christ's righteousness is imputed to all believers (Romans 3:21-28). 2 Corinthians 5:21 highlights the great exchange that takes place through the dying of Jesus whereby our sin is imputed to Him and His righteousness is imputed to those who will believe in Him.

Central to our salvation is the resurrection of Jesus because it shows that the Father accepted the payment that the Son made (John 10:18). As Jesus stands victorious over the grave, we stand justified before the Father (Romans 4:25). Jesus overcame death by resurrection (1 Corinthians 15:55). There was a demonstration of Christ's victory over Satan as well when Jesus rose from the dead, but only in the sense that Christ was shown to have undone the works of the devil (1 John 3:8), not that any ransom was paid to the devil.

Since there is no other representative and substitute who can take away sin, and since Jesus stood in our place once and for all, it is absolutely vital that we realize Jesus is the *only* Savior and that He is the *only* basis for the salvation of any sinner (Acts 4:12, Hebrews 7:25).

The work of Christ is complete and is able to save us completely (Hebrews 7:25). Jesus lived a full, righteous life on earth, obeying the Law of Moses and every demand of morality to the last jot and tittle (Matthew 5:17). In so doing, He demonstrated that He has a perfect righteousness that He is able to impute to those who are united to Him. When Jesus died on the cross, He did so as a substitute for those who are united with Him. Then, in the course of the life of each of these chosen ones, the Holy Spirit will apply this finished work of Christ to the life of the believer. That moment in time is the moment of regeneration. The whole process,

from election to glorification, can be called "salvation" (Titus 3:5).

CHAPTER 6

THE HOLY SPIRIT

We believe that the Holy Spirit, in all that He does, glorifies the Lord Jesus Christ. He convicts the world of its guilt. He regenerates sinners, and in Him they are baptized into union with Christ and adopted as heirs in the family of God. He also indwells, illuminates, guides, equips and empowers believers for Christ-like living and service.

—EFCA Statement of Faith

The Holy Spirit is the third member of the Trinity. He proceeds from the Father and the Son (Luke 11:13, John 14:16, 26). The Scripture refers to the Holy Spirit as "He" not "it", and He has attributes of personhood, such as grieving (Ephesians 4:30) and giving life (Genesis 1:2). As a Person, He can be obeyed (Acts 10:19-21), sinned against (Isaiah 63:10), and lied to (Acts 5:3). Lying to Him is lying to God (Acts 5:4).

There are both continuities and discontinuities between the Spirit's Old Testament and New Testament ministry. To the point of similarity, in both Testaments He is the eternal God who is present everywhere (Psalm 139:7, Acts 5:4) in all creation, which He had a role in creating (Genesis 1:2). To the point of differences, He now indwells all believers and exercises a stronger ministry in conforming believers into the image of the Son (Jeremiah 31:33, Ezekiel 36:26, 2 Corinthians 3:18). David worried that the Spirit might be taken from Him (Psalm 51:11), but the New Testament believer ought not (Ephesians 1:13-14).

So as not to leave us as orphans, Jesus sent another Counselor—the Holy Spirit—to be with us forever (John 14:18). The Holy Spirit seeks to bring honor to the name of Christ (John 16:14). Chief among the gifts with which He honors Christ is the presentation of a people (Titus 2:14) from every tribe, language, people and nation who are forever devoted to the praise of His name (Revelation 5:9). He creates a people for God by regenerating individuals, enabling them to believe in Christ (1 John 5:1). This new birth allows for us to be adopted members of this family of God (Romans 8:15, John 1:12). The Spirit glorifies the

Son by lifting the veil (2 Corinthians 3:17) in order for us to see the light of Christ's glory (2 Corinthians 4:4). By grace the Spirit regenerates the dead sinner, applying the redemption that was accomplished by Christ.

The Holy Spirit convicts the world of sin, righteousness, and judgment (John 16:8). The guilt of inherited sin and active choices made to sin would be rationalized away by all the people of the world were it not for the Spirit's convicting ministry (Romans 1:18). The Spirit quickens the conscience (Romans 2:15) to make people aware of their desperate need for Christ.

By sheer grace, the Spirit does not stop at making his elect aware of sin, but He actually gives to the elect a new heart (Deuteronomy 30:6), new eyes, and new ears (Deuteronomy 29:4) through which this new creation (2 Corinthians 5:17) is able to obey the gospel summons (Acts 17:30, 1 John 3:23). This act of regeneration is logically (if not chronologically) prior to faith. It is also biblically prior to faith because 1 John 5:1 puts being "born of God" antecedent to believing, in the same way John puts being "born of God" antecedent to practicing righteousness (1 John 2:29) and loving the brethren (1 John 4:7), things which accompany salvation (Hebrews 6:9) but are not the root of it (Galatians 5:22-23).

According to 1 Corinthians 12:13, the Spirit baptizes believers into the body of Christ, so that all Christians are members in the Church, having been brought together by the same baptism. The Spirit, from then on, dwells in each believer (John 7:37-39). But the believer demonstrates more or less evidence of this blessing because there are times when we are more or less filled with the Spirit (Ephesians 4:30, 5:18). Filling with the Holy Spirit means being surrendered to his control. To "walk by the Spirit" is obedience to Christ enabled by the Spirit. He helps us put to death the deeds of the flesh when we so walk (1 Corinthians 15:31).

The Spirit unites us with Christ. The phrase "in Christ" is found over ninety times in the New Testament. As the elect of God, even before regeneration, there were benefits of the believer's union with Christ intended for him, later to be applied. Jesus' death on the cross actually atoned for the believer's sin even though the believer had not yet been born (John 19:30). Christ's blood was specifically intended for the ones to whom repentance

(2 Timothy 2:25) and faith (Philippians 1:29) would later be granted.

Because of the adoption of the believer into the family of God, the believer is secured by the Spirit (Romans 8:15a). The Spirit causes us to pray to God as a child speaks to a father (Romans 8:15b). He bears witness inside of us that we belong in the family (Romans 8:16). And He reminds us of the inheritance awaiting us (Romans 8:17) in order to encourage us to suffer well until the time it is to be given.

The believers can see evidence of the work of the Spirit in the attitude we have and work we do which puts the spotlight on the glory and supremacy of Jesus Christ (John 16:14), not necessarily those things that appear most supernatural or dramatic. The Spirit's work through us is God-centered. Dependence on the Spirit is evidenced by godliness (Hebrews 10:29), not by might or power (Zechariah 4:6).

The gifts of the Holy Spirit (Romans 12:3-8, 1 Corinthians 12-14, 1 Peter 4:10-11, Ephesians 4:7-16) are manifestations of the Spirit for the common good of the Church. Most, but not all, continue throughout the church age. The persons occupying the office of Apostle (1 Corinthians 12:29) are referred to as gifts to the Church (Ephesians 4:11, 2:20), but the last of these persons died in the first century. The signs, wonders, and mighty works that authenticated an Apostle (2 Corinthians 12:12) are nowhere in Scripture said to have ceased, but these particular works ceased by virtue of there being no apostles left to authenticate. Whatever authentication of today's gospel witnesses may or may not take place, especially in frontier missions, is a matter left to God and the persons to whom the message appeared to be authenticated, but those reputed to be notable in this regard should not be given special status in the Church. The "anointing" referred to in 1 John 2:20 and 2:27 is a blessing of common knowledge that all Christians have, not secret gnostic knowledge available only to the initiated. In fact, denying the latter is why John brings up "the anointing".

The prophetic ministries of Agabus (Acts 11:27, 21:10-12) and prophetic utterances today (1 Corinthians 15:31-32, 1 Thessalonians 5:20) are not authoritative or binding, whereas everything written in Scripture is authoritative and binding.

These higher gifts of prophecy and teaching (1 Corinthians 12:31, 14:1), higher than tongues for the reason of intelligibility (1 Corinthians 14:2), are important for building up the Church. A church without at least one gifted preacher or teacher is sure to languish (2 Timothy 2:2). Gifts of healing, helping, and administrating (1 Corinthians 12:28) are also to be desired. Lastly, tongues is to be desired for the enrichment of personal prayer times (1 Corinthians 14:18), but since, in the absence of Apostolic ministry, we ostensibly have no one to interpret tongues, 1 Corinthians 14:28 applies, and tongues should not be spoken in any church setting or anywhere outside of privacy with God alone.

The gifts of the Spirit are not as good an indicator of spiritual health (or of spiritual life) as the fruit of the Spirit (Galatians 5:22-23)—of which love is preeminent (1 Corinthians 13:13). The fruit of the Spirit has to do with character traits that come out as the believer is conformed into the image of Christ (Romans 12:1-2). Gifts of the Spirit have to do with God empowering and equipping believers to do certain work, especially in the Church (1 Corinthians 12), but also at large, such as evangelism (Ephesians

4:11). The fruit of the Spirit and the gifts of the Spirit function in the life of every genuine child of God.

CHAPTER 7

THE CHURCH

We believe that the true church comprises all who have been justified by God's grace through faith alone in Christ alone. They are united by the Holy Spirit in the body of Christ, of which He is the Head. The true church is manifest in local churches, whose membership should be composed only of believers. The Lord Jesus mandated two ordinances, baptism and the Lord's Supper, which visibly and tangibly express the gospel. Though they are not the means of salvation, when celebrated by the church in genuine faith, these ordinances confirm and nourish the believer.
—EFCA Statement of Faith

To be justified is to be declared righteous, in a forensic sense (Romans 3:26). No one has the ability to earn actual righteousness (Romans 1:18-3:19). Thus, justification is entirely a gift of grace. Men contribute nothing. But that does not mean that God cannot use means to justify us. He has, in fact, done so. He uses our faith, which is both something we exercise (we place our trust in Him) and, at the same time, something He gives (Ephesians 2:8-9). Faith is taking God at His Word (Hebrews 11). Our creaturely will surrenders to the Lordship of Christ, but it only does so when His grace draws us (John 6:44). Grace is unmerited favor. Salvation is by faith in order that it might rest on grace (Romans 4:16). Since His grace (not our faith, much less our love) is the very ground floor of our salvation, the Bible calls the gospel the "gospel of grace" (Acts 20:24), but nowhere does Scripture call it "the gospel of faith" or "the gospel of love". Christ alone is the object of the faith that God gives (Philippians 1:29), that we also exercise, so we are saved by the "gospel of Christ" (Romans 1:16, Mark 1:1). Unless Christ is the object of faith, that faith is not saving, because Christ alone is Savior. He alone can save and include us in the true Church.

The Church is thus the makeup of all Christians. The Church is the "body of Christ" (1 Corinthians 12), meaning that Jesus is the Lord (Master, Ruler) and "Head" (Leader) of the Church, and she functions as a unified organism under His direction. There is no episcopal leader over the Church. Christ alone rules the Church.

Believers are connected to one another and under the headship of Christ. The Church is "the bride of Christ", meaning that He has a special love for her, redeems her with His sacrifice, and washes her with His Word (Ephesians 5:25-33).

Christ is Head over the "true Church", also known as the "Church invisible", which is made up of all true believers everywhere, but Christ is also the Head of every "local church". The local church is a called-out assembly who gather (Acts 2:42-44, Heb. 10:25) for the purpose of hearing the Word (2 Timothy 4:2), partaking of the ordinances (Matthew 28:19, 1 Corinthians 11:24), practicing church discipline (Matthew 18:15-20), and worshipping (John 4:23).

The local church needs to be a "believer's church", not a loose association of whoever happens to show up, because the Church is a body with functions to perform, including decision-making that has consequences (Matthew 18:15-20). Membership is important because it identifies who "the majority" (2 Corinthians 2:6) is. Members have a responsibility to contribute their time, talents and treasure to the church to which they belong.

Congregationalism is the best ecclesiological arrangement because each individual church governs itself in direct submission to Christ as Head (Colossians 1:18). When there is no governing authority from the outside that dictates what she must do, the church is free to make her stand upon the Word (Ephesians 6:13). Congregationalism is important because it honors the priesthood of all believers (1 Peter 2:9) and the Scriptures that speak to the will of the majority (2 Co. 2:6).

At Cornerstone Church, congregational rule involves elders exercising leadership and ruling authority, but not in a dictatorial way (1 Peter 5:1-4). The congregation votes on major decisions. Elders, who are also pastors and overseers, lead the ministry and care for the spiritual lives of the congregants (Acts 20:17, 28). Deacons (from the Greek "dia", meaning "thorough", and "konis", meaning "dust") are servants who are so fast and active in their serving that they kick up a cloud of dust in their wake. They "wait on tables" (Acts 6:2) in order to free up the elders to focus on the ministry of the Word and of prayer.

Congregationalism does not mean that each local church is a loner. "An association and fellowship of autonomous but interdependent congregations of like faith and congregational government", like the EFCA, demonstrates that there are good ways for churches to be independent yet help one another though prayer, encouragement, and joint efforts in ministry. Within the local church, under Christ, the highest authority is the congregation itself (Matthew 18:17, Acts 6:3). But congregations themselves willingly participate with other congregations that are like-minded, especially those that fully subscribe to the same Statement of Faith, as all EFCA churches do.

Water baptism itself doesn't save, but "baptism saves" (1 Peter 3:21), not in the moment or act of immersion, but in a symbolic sense, as it pictures the new birth and regeneration of the Holy Spirit (Titus 3:5). Although water baptism is not necessary for salvation, it is a very important (Romans 6:1-11) ordinance. Except in the case of physical incapability, sprinkling or other modes of baptism, besides immersion, should not be done because immersion alone communicates the metaphor of being buried with Christ and raised to newness of life (Romans 6:1-5). It would be sinful to refuse to be baptized, because baptism is clearly commanded (Matthew 28:29, Acts 2:38).

Likewise, the Lord's Supper is an important ordinance for the Lord's people. It is not a meal for unregenerate people, but is to be taken with reverence, and with an examination of one's own heart, by believers (1 Corinthians 11:28). Unlike the singularity of baptism, it should be celebrated regularly (1 Corinthians 11:25). It symbolizes the new covenant, which was promised in the Old Testament (Ezekiel 36:26, Jeremiah 31:31) and of which Jesus spoke when He broke the bread and passed the cup (Luke 22:20). The Roman Catholic understanding of transubstantiation does violence to the finished work of Christ (1 John 2:2). The Lutheran understanding edges too close to the Roman Catholic position. The Zwinglian view of the Lord's Table, involving the real presence of Christ but not magically in the elements, is near the point of what Christ taught (Mark 14:22-25, Luke 22:18-20). The elements are representative of Christ.

Baptism, ideally, ought to take place before one begins to take the Lord's Supper. A believer who refuses to be baptized is disobeying Christ (Acts 2:38), so examination of the heart (1 Corinthians 11:28) should bring conviction to be baptized. However, if a child has made a credible profession of faith in Jesus and asks to be baptized, but a parent withholds baptism, not on the grounds that the child might not be saved but on the conviction that the child is too young to draw on the memory of their baptism for the rest of life (Romans 6:3), the parent should not withhold the Lord's Table. The difference between baptism and the Lord's Table at this point is that the former is a once-in-a-lifetime event, the memory of which becomes significant for the rest of life (Romans 6:11-14). Conversely, the saved child should not be denied that latter way of drawing nearer to Christ, unless it is the child who is unwilling to be baptized. We must guard the Table, but we must also remember that Christ warns us to forbid not the children from coming to Him (Matthew 19:14), and that would include not hindering their sincere desire to draw nearer to Christ through obedience to Him in remembering Him at His Table.

Both baptism and the Lord's Table are gifts and a means of grace. They don't magically confer grace, but God blesses faithful obedience to what He ordained. The worshipper draws near to God and can experience a cleansing of conscience.

Baptism and the Lord's Supper confirm believers in the Faith by granting a public recognition by the church that they are regarded as being regenerate (Acts 10:47). Christ uses these means

within His sovereign plan to nourish believers, centering our minds

on the Lord we love (1 Corinthians 11:23-25).

CHAPTER 8

CHRISTIAN LIVING

We believe that God's justifying grace must not be separated from His sanctifying power and purpose. God commands us to love Him supremely and others sacrificially, and to live out our faith with care for one another, compassion toward the poor and justice for the oppressed. With God's Word, the Spirit's power, and fervent prayer in Christ's name, we are to combat the spiritual forces of evil. In obedience to Christ's commission, we are to make disciples among all people, always bearing witness to the gospel in word and deed.

—EFCA Statement of Faith

Sanctification is the process of being set apart from the world and conformed into the likeness of Christ (2 Corinthians 3:18). While sanctification can be spoken of positionally, meaning that in Christ we *have been* set apart (Hebrews 10:10), it must not be conflated with justification (Romans 3:24), which is a forensic declaration and not a process. Sanctification happens by the activity of the

Holy Spirit in our lives, especially as we yield our will to His control. Sanctification is not optional for Christians. We are commanded to be holy, set apart from sin, set apart to serve God (1 Peter 1:13-21, 2 Peter 3:18).

The works of a believer must demonstrate that his faith is not a vain (1 Corinthians 15:2), dead (James 2:26) faith. Works are the fruit of lively faith (Ephesians 2:10). They function to glorify our God and Father in heaven (Matthew 5:16) and bless others (Luke 6:28), especially the household of the faith (Galatians 6:10). Works make no contribution to justification (Ephesians 2:8-9).

Assurance of salvation is provided by the Spirit of God (Romans 8:16) to the believer. The discipline of the Father over the life of the one He accepts as a child (Hebrews 12:4-11) is not pleasant, and the wayward child may doubt his sonship for a time (Luke 15:19), but God will encourage him to lift his drooping hands and strengthen his weak knees (Hebrews 12:12). It is God's grace that guarantees the perseverance of the saints (Ephesians 1:13-14).

Love for God is preeminent in the Christian life because God is above all things (Isaiah 55:9), He acts for His own sake (Isaiah

43:25), and He commands us to act for His sake (Matthew 22:37). The first table of the Law reflects this preeminent concern, since they are vertical commands about how we are to relate to Him. God tolerates no idolatry (Romans 1:23, Jeremiah 2:11), because He is jealous for His own glory (Exodus 20:5).

We love God because He first loved us (1 John 4:19). This order is important, because unless God's love is shed abroad into our hearts (Romans 5:5), our hearts would be loveless and cold (Ezekiel 11:19). Love for God runs over the cup of the believer's heart to touch other people (Psalm 23:5). From the inexhaustible fountain of God's love, the believer, who rightly drinks from the fountain (Psalm 36:9), is able even to love enemies (Matthew 5:44).

To live out one's faith means to put Christian principles into action. A so-called faith that does not result in good works is no saving faith at all (James 1:26, 2:14) and is useless. Christians are recipients of "the faith"—Christianity, which was once-for-all handed down to us (Jude 1:3). The reception of the faith carries with it a responsibility to adorn it (Titus 2:10) with good works (Ephesians 2:10). Living by faith is keeping one's eyes set on

Christ (Hebrews 12:1-3) and doing that which is pleasing to Him (1 John 3:22).

We are commanded to do good to all men, and especially to those who belong to the household of the faith (Galatians 6:10). Every Christian is to function within the context of a local body of believers (1 Corinthians 12) and treat one another the way we would want to be treated (Matthew 7:12). We are to encourage one another and build one another up (1 Thessalonians 5:11). We have a continuing debt to love one another (Romans 13:8, 1 Corinthians 13).

Regenerate people ought to have compassion for the poor, meeting needs where we can (Ephesians 2:10, Galatians 2:10). We should help to pursue justice for those who have been wronged. We should work to prevent injustice, especially rescuing babies from the slaughterhouse that is the abortion industry in this country (Leviticus 18:21). With compassion, the Church ought to help widows who are widows indeed (1 Timothy 5:5). Orphans should likewise be recipients of the Church's special care (James 1:27). Victims of unjust government and other disenfranchised persons who suffer at the hands of evil people should find the church to be a friend and comfort (Isaiah 1:17), but victimization is never to be assumed, nor should all claims of victimization be affirmed (Proverbs 18:17). Deceitful political ideologies, such as Critical Race Theory, falsely impute guilt, libeling people as "oppressors". These oppressive ideologies need to be resisted. Local churches are called to be salt and light in the culture (Matthew 5:13-14). Focusing on the gospel does not imply silence in the face of injustice.

Our ultimate enemies are not people or human government, but spiritual forces of evil (Ephesians 6:12). By wielding the sword of the Spirit (Ephesians 6:17, Luke 4:1-13), by fervent and persevering prayer (Ephesians 6:18-20), and by the power of the Spirit (Zechariah 4:6, Romans 8:26), we overcome the enemy in spiritual warfare (1 John 4:1-6).

The command to make disciples who are obedient (Matthew 28:19) identifies the central mission of the Church. Whereas ministries of compassion and justice primarily address issues of temporal concern, the transfer of an eternal soul out of the domain of darkness into the Kingdom of Light (1 Peter 2:9) is a transaction of eternal significance. Evangelism is the first activity in making disciples. Christ-centered preaching of the Word (Galatians 3:1), speaking of Christ with unbelievers in the ordinary flow of life (Luke 24:15), and intentional designs to bring the gospel to people (Acts 13:1-3) are all important means of evangelism. Those who are reached with the Gospel should be taught the whole counsel of God (Acts 20:27). Discipleship should also include sharing one's life and modeling an example of the Christian life (1 Thessalonians 2:8).

The scope of the Great Commission is "all people". This implies that local churches ought to be ambitious to take the gospel to people groups that do not have many who know Christ (Romans 15:20). Sending missionaries must remain a high priority (Romans 10:15). In a given locality, witnessing should be indiscriminate with regard to ethnicity, gender, sexuality, economics, nationality, etc. The gospel is to be issued to all people without distinction. We ought to be colorblind in the local churches and in all our efforts at disciple making (Colossians 3:11).

The gospel is the good news about the person and work of Jesus Christ. Entailments of the gospel, such as how we are to live as Christians, are not to be conflated with the gospel itself. The

Great Commandment (Matthew 22:36) is only law without the gospel. It condemns (Romans 3:20) and cannot save. But the gospel saves (Titus 3:5-7) and frees the Christian to obey the Great Commandment from a transformed heart (Romans 6:17). Deeds of mercy and compassion flow from a transformed heart (Galatians 2:10). The "social gospel", which is no gospel at all (Galatians 1:6-9), conflates law and gospel by trying to do the former and jettison the latter, while still using the latter in its jargon. It is a misnomer. Conversely, it is a mistake to neglect the whole counsel of God (Acts 20:27) by refusing all social engagement to focus all energy on the gospel. German Pietism may have had an unintended effect in this direction, but good works in society should follow the gospel (Ephesians 2:10).

The gospel cannot be preached without words, since the gospel is a message. But deeds done by Christians can adorn the message we preach (1 Peter 3:3-4). The world will notice the way Christians live, either for the good (Matthew 5:16), which glorifies God, or for the bad (2 Peter 2:2), which causes disrepute. Caring for the homeless, rescuing those enslaved by the sex trade, calling out to women as they enter an abortion clinic to plead with them for the life of their children, helping people transition back into life after imprisonment, tutoring struggling kids in an after-school program, and similar loving deeds are adornment for the gospel (Titus 2:10).

CHAPTER 9

CHRIST'S RETURN

We believe in the personal, bodily and premillennial return of our Lord Jesus Christ. The coming of Christ, at a time known only to God, demands constant expectancy and, as our blessed hope, motivates the believer to godly living, sacrificial service and energetic mission.

—EFCA Statement of Faith

God has promised that Christ will return to earth in the same way He left (Acts 1:11). Seven years prior to His physical decent from heaven, He will catch the church up into heaven to be with Him forever (1 Thessalonians 4:16). This rapture is imminent (1 Thessalonians 5:2). After the rapture, a 7-year period of tribulation will overtake the earth (Revelation 6-19). After the tribulation, Christ will reign in peace for 1,000 years, while the devil is bound (Rev. 20:1-10). The devil will then be released for a final deception before the Great White Throne Judgment (Revelation 20:11-15) and the ushering in of the eternal state (Revelation 21-22), where the wicked perish in everlasting punishment and the righteous enjoy heaven.

These events are taught in the Scriptures, the book of Revelation in particular, and should not be explained away by appeals to symbolism. The literal interpretation of Revelation results in a premillennial view of end times, over against the postmillennial view, where the Millennium is a period where the Church makes things better in the world to usher in the return of Christ and the Tribulation is often regarded in preterist terms as a bygone persecution. This is also over against the amillennial view, where the present Church age is the Millennium (figuratively speaking) such that no future 1,000 period is to be expected and the Tribulation is understood in terms of the sufferings of this present age. Views other than the premillennial one fail due to overly symbolic interpretation and the failure to see the promises made to Israel literally fulfilled (Genesis 12:1-3, Isaiah 11:6-16). One of the strengths of the postmillennial position is that it tends to motivate the Church to be active in seeking to transform the world. One of the strengths of the amillennial view is that it carries with it much of the weight of the Reformation tradition.

Christ's return will be personal because He Himself promised to return (John 14:3). Moreover, He must fulfill the yet-unfulfilled prophecies of Messiah's coming, such as Isaiah 11:6-16. His return will be bodily because the incarnation was an eternal union of the divine nature and human nature, so He must return in the body (John 1:14). His return will be glorious in that Christ Himself is the radiance of the glory of God (Hebrews 1:3) and to see His face is to see the Light of His glory (2 Corinthians 4:4).

The relationship between Israel and the Church involves both continuities and discontinuities. The Church can be called the Israel of God (Galatians 6:16), yet, even in the Church age, Israel remains an ethnic people with whom God upholds special promises. While a remnant of the Jews have believed the gospel and belong to the Church, a partial hardening has happened to ethnic Israel (Romans 11:25). Before the Second Coming of

Christ, there will be a massive revival among the Jews whereby "all Israel will be saved" (Romans 11:26). The promise of the New Covenant (Ezekiel 36:26) thus applies in a special way to ethnic Israel.

Jesus sits on the throne at the Father's right hand in heaven (Psalm 110:1), but he will soon come to sit on David's throne as the King over Israel (2 Samuel 7:12), seated in present day Jerusalem (Zechariah 14:4). He will rule the whole world when the Kingdom is established on earth (Zechariah 14:9). Until that time, there is a sense in which the Kingdom is already here, because Jesus did not leave the Church as orphans (John 14:18), but reigns spiritually by the work of the Holy Spirit in the Church, indwelling every believer (Luke 17:21).

We do not know the time of Christ's return, so attempts to prognosticate such things are immodest (Matthew 24:36). We should instead live in "constant expectancy", since He could come to snatch us away at any instant (1 Thessalonians 4:17). The parable of the foolish virgin demands that we be watchful for His coming (Matthew 25:13). We should be ready, meaning that the talents we are given to steward ought always be put to good use until His coming (Matthew 25:14-30). The return of Christ is our blessed hope (Titus 2:13), since we know that we cannot bring utopia to the earth without Him, and besides, it is He Himself we desire most (Revelation 22:4-5, 22:16). Wanting to be found good and faithful at His appearing, which is itself a promise we love (2 Timothy 4:8, Matthew 25:23), we are motivated to godly living, sacrificial service, and energetic mission.

CHAPTER 10

RESPONSE AND ETERNAL DESTINY

We believe that God commands everyone everywhere to believe the gospel by turning to Him in repentance and receiving the Lord Jesus Christ. We believe that God will raise the dead bodily and judge the world, assigning the unbeliever to condemnation and eternal conscious punishment and the believer to eternal blessedness and joy with the Lord in the new heaven and the new earth, to the praise of His glorious grace. Amen.

—EFCA Statement of Faith

The gospel is the message of the gracious saving work of God in Jesus Christ: that the Father gave the Son of God to die for sins and rise from the dead in order that believing ones will have forgiveness of sin and eternal life (John 3:16). Having faith is the only thing we must "do" to be saved (John 6:29, Ephesians 2:8-9), and Jesus is the only Gate (John 10:9) in whom we place our trust (Romans 10:11). The gospel is a message that is to be universally offered to all (Revelation 22:17), but only believers will be saved and remain with Jesus forever (John 14:6).

Believing is the only requirement for salvation because it is entirely empty-handed. The one who trusts brings no good thing to the table. That is what makes believing the fit counterpart to grace, which is entirely unmerited favor (Romans 4:16, 11:6). Faith is an instrument God uses in us (Philippians 1:29) as means through which He imputes His righteousness (Isaiah 61:10).

The reverse side of faith is repentance. Repentance is turning away from sin by turning to Christ (Mark 1:15, Acts 20:21). Repentance is itself a gift from God (2 Timothy 2:24-26). It is a necessary aspect of saving faith, because Christ makes it plain that one must take up his cross and follow Him (Matthew 16:24), not just make an intellectual affirmation regarding the facts of the gospel.

To receive the Son of God is synonymous with believing (John 1:12, Romans 10:9-10). It conveys the idea of accepting the command to place full trust in Him, while turning away from sin

(Mark 1:15, Acts 20:21). Obeying the command to believe is the only way to be saved (1 Corinthians 15:1-2). Conversely, disobeying the command all the way through death and therefore spurning the testimony of the Spirit (John 16:14) results in eternal condemnation (Revelation 20:11-15).

The gospel is good news regarding the person and work of the Son, and those given these glad tidings are immediately commanded to repent and believe (Acts 17:30, Romans 1:5). Disobeying the command to believe is further condemnation against the unbeliever who already stands condemned on account of sins (John 3:18, Romans 1:18).

As Jesus rose bodily from the dead (Matthew 28:6) and will return bodily (Acts 1:11), believers will be resurrected bodily (1 Corinthians 15:12) to everlasting life, and unbelievers will be resurrected bodily (Revelation 20:12) to everlasting punishment. The body is therefore an important aspect of humanity, and bodies are not to be regarded dualistically.

The Great White Throne Judgment (Revelation 20:11-15) will be God's appraisal of the works of unbelievers, all of whom will be found wanting. By contrast, the Bema—the Judgement Seat of

Christ—will be an examination of the lives of believers for the purpose of issuing rewards (Romans 14:10-12, 2 Corinthians 5:10, 1 Corinthians 3:12-15). Those whose names appear in the Lamb's Book of Life (Revelation 13:8) will escape being measured according to the books of works (Revelation 20:11-15).

The burning away of character flaws at the Bema—the Judgment Seat of Christ (1 Corinthians 3:12-15)—is not a purging of the believer's sin where the sinner is punished for bad works. Since the believer's sin was answered for by Jesus, there is no such thing as Purgatory. Indeed, there is no shame. Rather, impurities are burned away in the fire of Christ's holiness (Hebrews 12:29). The believer is separated from the sin nature and will forever go and sin no more (John 8:11). There will be no condemnation for the believer who stands before the Bema (Romans 8:1), because all condemnation for the believer's sin was laid upon Christ and finished with His death on the cross (John 19:30).

Unbelievers will suffer hell. Hell is eternal conscious punishment, which means there is no annihilation (Matthew 25:46), but the unbeliever suffers forever and is aware of that suffering and the reason for it. This second death (Revelation

20:14) involves continued sinful rage against God, but no outlet in God's created world to find any delight in expressing that rage, or in using it to influence others. The unevangelized also stand condemned because they are also sinners (Romans 1:18ff), which makes missions not only necessary but exceedingly urgent (Romans 9:3). God ordains the means to an end as well as the end itself, so He gets the glory for missions.

The first death, unlike the second, is not an eternal loss, but is a separation of body and spirit. The spirits of those outside of Christ go to a holding place (1 Peter 3:19) to await judgment. The spirits of those who are in Christ (Ephesians 1:1-14), absent from the body, are immediately with Christ (2 Corinthians 5:8), awaiting reunification with the body (1 Thess. 4:17). Even before the New Jerusalem descends upon the New Heaven and New Earth at a time yet future (Revelation 21:1-22:5), believers experience life (John 11:26) and heaven (Revelation 21:10) at the very moment of physical death.

The New Heaven and New Earth are not the same as the Millennial reign of Christ. The Millennium takes place on this earth in Garden-of-Eden-like living conditions (Isaiah 11:6-16). The world will see what a difference it makes to have a righteous King over Israel and over the world (Zechariah 14:4, 9). After the return of Christ and His thousand-year reign on earth, all humankind will be assembled before God's Great White Throne. All believers, already safely on His right, and all unbelievers, now positioned on His left, will be judged (Rev. 20:11-15, Matt. 25:32). Believers enter immediately into heaven by the merits of Christ. Unbelievers are judged by their works, which prove wanting, and they are cast into hell with the devil and his angels (Revelation 20:15). God then re-creates a perfect New Heaven and New Earth, where there is no sin, not even a tinge of sin or death, and where we live there to worship forever (Rev. 21-22).

At this point, having considered ten areas of theology, it is fitting to conclude the discussion with a doxological note, centered on God. All true theology redounds to the praise of God's glorious grace (Ephesians 1:6). "The grace of the Lord Jesus be with all. Amen" (Revelation 22:21).

Made in the USA
Middletown, DE
13 April 2021